Chicken Jokes:

110+
Chicken
Jokes for kids

JENNY KELLETT

The Chicken Joke Book for Kids

www.bellanovabooks.com

Copyright 2023 by Jenny Kellett, all rights reserved. Copyright and other intellectual property laws protect these materials. Reproduction or retransmission of the materials, in whole or in part, in any manner, without the prior written consent of the copyright holder, is a violation of copyright law.

Which day of the week do chickens hate the most?

Fry-Day!

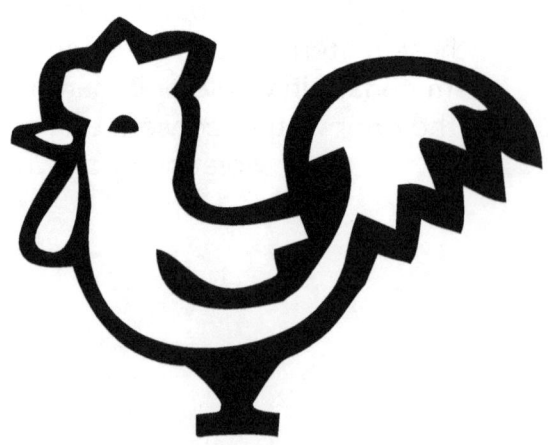

Did you hear about the chicken who could only lay eggs in the winter?

She was no spring chicken!

Why didn't the chicken cross the road?

Because they were chicken!

What do you call a group of chickens clucking in unison?

A hen-semble.

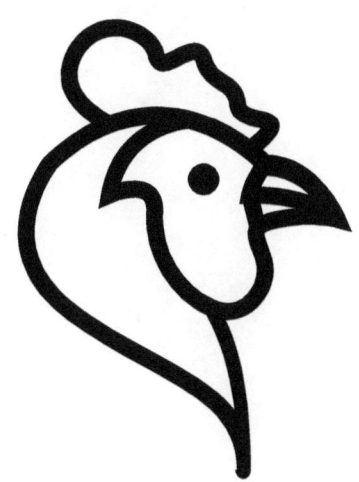

What do chickens serve at birthday parties?

Coop-cakes!

What do chicken families do on Saturday afternoon?

They go on peck-nics!

What do you call a crazy chicken?

A cuckoo-cluck!

What does an alarm cluck say?

"Tick-tock-a-doodle-doo!"

What do you call the outside of a hand gren-egg?

The bomb-shell!

What do you call a chicken in a shellsuit?

An egg!

How do chickens bake a cake?

From scratch!

What happened to the baby chicken that misbehaved at school?

It was eggspelled.

Why did the chicken stand in the middle of the road?

Because he wanted to play squash!

Why did the piece of gum cross the road?

Because it was stuck to the chicken's foot!

Why did the rooster cross the road?

To cockadoodle dooo something!

What do you call a joke book for chickens?

A yolk book!

What did the baby chicken say when he saw his mother sitting on an orange?

Dad, dad, look what mama-laid!

What happens when a hen eats gunpowder?

She lays hand gren-eggs!

What do you call a bird that's afraid to fly?

Chicken!

Why did the chicken cross the road, roll in the mud and cross the road again?

Because he was a dirty double-crosser.

Why did the chicken go to KFC?

To see his brother!

Why did the chicken cross the playground?

To get to the other slide.

What do you call a rooster who wakes you up at the same time every morning?

An alarm cluck!

What do you get when you cross a chicken and a four-leaf clover?

The Cluck o'the Irish!

What happened to the chicken whose feathers were all pointing the wrong way?

She was tickled to death!

What do you call a scary chicken?

A poultry-geist.

Why did Beethoven kill his chicken?

It kept saying "Bach, Bach, Bach..."

How long do chickens work?

Around the cluck!

Why did the Roman chicken cross the road?

She was afraid someone would Caesar!

How does a chicken mail a letter to her friend?

In a HEN-velope!

Why does a rooster watch TV?

For hen-tertainment!

What do you call a witch who likes the beach but is scared of the water?

A chicken sand-witch!

What do call a chicken that got too close to a nuclear plant?

Atomic cluck.

What does a chicken wipe his beak with?

A henkerchief!

What time do chickens go to lunch?

Twelve o cluck!

What do you call a frightened scuba diver?

Chicken of the sea!

What do you get when you cross a dog with a chicken?

A hen that lays pooched eggs.

Why did the chicken cross the internet?

It wanted to get to the other site!

When fruit comes from a fruit tree, what kind of tree does a chicken come from?

A poul-tree!

Which dance will a chicken not do?

The foxtrot!

What do you get if you cross a Land Rover with a baby chicken?

A 'Jeep-Jeep'!

What is Superchicken's real identity?

Cluck Kent.

How do you know when a chicken is under arrest?

She's wearing hen-cuffs.

Why did the turkey cross the road?

To prove he wasn't a chicken!

What do you get when you cross a chicken with a duck?

A bird that lays down!

If the rooster laid an egg on a roof, which way would the egg roll?

Nowhere, because roosters don't lay eggs!

What do you get when a chicken lays an egg on top of a barn?

An eggroll!

What do you call someone who steals chicken?

A Chicken Pot Pirate.

When is chicken soup not good for your health?

When you're a chicken!

Why did the T-rex cross the road?

Because the chicken hadn't evolved yet!

Why did the chicken cross the road half way?

He wanted to lay it on the line!

Why don't chickens like people?

They beat eggs!

What's a haunted chicken?

A poultry-geist!

Which side of a chicken has the most feathers?

The outside!

Why did the chicken cross the road?
To get to your house.

Knock Knock
Who's there?

The chicken!

Why did the chicken cross the basketball court?

He heard the referee calling fowls.

How did the eggs leave the highway?

They used the eggs-it.

What do chickens grow on?

Eggplants!

What does an evil hen lay?

Deviled eggs!

Why did the chicken cross the road?

To prove to the possum that it could be done!

What does a confused hen lay?

Scrambled eggs!

What did the sick chicken say?

"I have the people-pox!"

Silly girl: Why does your son say, "Cluck, cluck, cluck".

Mrs. Poulet: Because he thinks he's a chicken.

Silly girl: Why don't you tell him he's not a chicken?

Mrs. Poulet: Because we need the eggs.

Why did the rooster run away?

He was chicken!

Why did the rubber chicken cross the road?

Because she wanted to stretch her legs.

Why did the chick disappoint his mother?

He wasn't what he was cracked up to be!

Why does a chicken coop have two doors?

Because if had four doors it would be a chicken sedan!

What do you call a chicken crossing the road?

Poultry in motion!

Why do hens lay eggs?

If they dropped them, they'd break!

How did the egg get up the mountain?

It scrambled up!

What did the Spanish egg farmer say to his hens?

Oh lay!

Why did the chicken go cluck cluck cluck?

Because it's a chicken, d'uh!

Why did the chicken lift weights?

She needed the egg-ercise!

What do you get if you cross a chicken with a cement mixer?

A brick layer!

Why did the chicken skeleton cross the road?

Because he didn't have the guts.

What do you call it when it rains chickens and ducks?

Fowl weather!

Why do chickens rinse out their mouths with soap?

Because they are fowl-mouthed!

Which came first, chicken or egg?

Chicken. Check it out in the dictionary!

What did one chicken say to the other as they walked through poison ivy?

If I scratch your back, you scratch mine

How many eggs does it take to screw in a lightbulb?

None - eggs don't have hands!

How do baby chickens dance?

Chick-to-chick.

Why did the chicken cross the beach?

To get to the other tide.

Why did the chicken cross the state line?

To get out of Kentucky.

What Am I?

I'm found on a farm but I'm not a tractor

I can be roasted but I'm not a peanut

I have feathers but I'm not a pillow

I'm fowl but I'm not disgusting

I lay eggs but I'm not an ostrich

Answer: *A chicken!*

Why did the turkey cross the road?

It was the chicken's day off!

What did Snow White call her chicken?

Egg White

Who tells the best chicken jokes?

Comedi-hens!

Psychiatrist: What seems to be the problem?
Patient: I think I'm a chicken.
Psychiatrist: How long as this been going on?
Patient: Ever since I came out of my shell.

Why is it easy for chicks to talk?

Because talk is cheep!

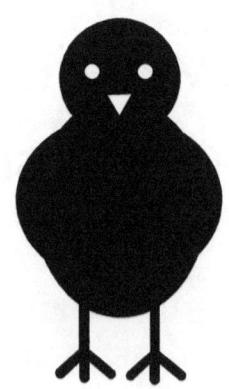

What do chickens call a school test?

Eggs-amination

Who wrote the book, 'Great Egg-spectations'?

Charles Chickens

Knock knock
Who's there?

Chicken
Chicken who?

Chicken your pockets, maybe your keys are in there!

What do you get if you cross a cocker spaniel, a poodle and a rooster?

Cockerpoodledoo!

What happens when you drop a hand gren-egg?

It eggs-plodes!

What do you get if you cross a chicken with a cow?

Roost beef!

Knock knock
Who's there?

Chicken
Chicken who?

Just chicken to see who's home!

Where do tough chickens come from?

Hard-boiled eggs!

How do comedians like their eggs?

Funny side up!

What do you call a city of 20 million eggs?

New Yolk City

Why did McDonald's run out of chicken McNuggets?

The farmer counted his chickens before they hatched!

What does a chicken need to lay an egg every day?

Hendurance

What is a chicken's favorite tree?

A y-oak tree!

What do you get when you cross a Barbie and a grill?

Barbie-q Chicken!

Where do chickens like to go on vacation?

SandiEGGo!

What do you call the door to a chicken barn?

The hen-trance

Where do you find a chicken with no legs?

Exactly where you left it!

What's the most musical part of a chicken?

The drumstick!

A chicken was going to America and his friend was asked where he was going.

He said "I don't know where he is going, but I do know he is not going to Kentucky."

How can you drop an egg six feet without breaking it?

By dropping it 7 feet – it won't break for the first six!

How do monsters like their eggs?

Terrified!

What do you call a mischievous egg?

A practical yolker!

What do you get when you cross a chicken with a martian?

An eggs-traterrestrial!

Where are chicks born?

In Chick-ago!

What do you call an enthusiastic chicken?

Hen-thusiastic.

What does the chicken say to get across a busy street?

Eggs-scuse me please!

How do you know if it's too hot in the chicken pen?

The chickens are laying hard-boiled eggs.

How many eggs can you eat on an empty stomach?

One, because then your stomach won't be empty anymore!

Why did the chicken cross the hay field?

To get to the other scythe!

Visit us at

www.bellanovabooks.com

for more great joke books, and more!

www.ingramcontent.com/pod-product-compliance
Lightning Source LLC
LaVergne TN
LVHW040154080526
838202LV00042B/3161